# NORTHWEST ECOLOG

## LAWRENCE FERLINGHETTI

## City Lights Books

Drawings by the author after Hokusai & Ben Shahn

Cover: Haida sea monster

Ecolog: based upon Allen Ginsberg's coinage of "ecologue" (in *The Fall of America*), a fusion of the Greek eclogue & ecology.

"Reading Apollinaire by the Rogue River" first was printed on the Op/Ed page of the *Los Angeles Times*. "At the Public Market" first appeared on the front page of the *Seattle Post Intelligencer*.

Library of Congress Cataloging in Publication Data

Ferlinghetti, Lawrence.
    Northwest ecolog.

    I. Title.
PS3511.E557N6      811'.5'4      78-2627
ISBN 0-87286-102-3

CITY LIGHTS BOOKS are published at the City Lights Bookstore, Columbus & Broadway, San Francisco, California 94133.

# CONTENTS

Found these two new shiny poems lying by the river on our first morning by the Deschutes:

# THE OLD SAILORS

On the green riverbank
                 age late fifties
I am beginning
        to remind myself
of my great Uncle Désir
            in the Virgin Islands
On a Saint Thomas back beach
he lived when I last saw him
in a small shack
          under the palms
Eighty years old
          straight as a Viking
  (where the Danes once landed)
he stood looking out
           over the flat sea
  blue eyes or grey
          with the sea in them
salt upon his lashes
         We
        were always sea wanderers
No salt here now
         by the great river
    in the high desert range
Old sailors stranded
      the steelhead
        they too lost without it
          leap up and die

# WILD LIFE CAMEO, EARLY MORN

By the great river Deschutes
        on the meadowbank greensward
  sun just hitting
        the high bluffs
  stone cliffs sculpted
        high away
    across the river

At the foot of a steep brown slope
        a mile away
  six white-tail deer
  four young bucks with branched antlers
    and two small does
        mute in eternity
        drinking the river
then in real time raising heads
  and climbing up and up
        a steep faint switchback
    into full sun

I bring them close in the binoculars
        as in a round cameo
  There is a hollow bole in a tree
        one looks into
  One by one they
    drink silence
        (the two does last)

one by one
        climb up so calm
                over the rim of the canyon
   and without looking back
                        disappear forever

Like certain people
          in my life

*7 August 77*

In the dark funky old wooden Maupin Hotel bar / while
we're in the two-block-long town for supplies / get a beer
called Blitz and perch on a stool next to the raunchy locals /
fishhooks in their redneck panama cowboy hats / It's five PM
and the daily blitz is on / I'm baked from the sun on the river
and soak up two Blitzes in a minute / Listening to the enter-
taining conversation along the bar / The wino next to me is
staring at a fly on the woodwork / 'I'm gonna kill that fucken
fly' he mumbles darkly / trying to focus on it / Next to him is
this old geezer with a hearing-aid / 'Yeah' says the old geezer
'Flies is the oney thing that works on the steelhead!' / The first
guy is still contemplating the fly on the bar / 'That fucken fly
is got to die' he whispers, very morose / 'Yeah' says the old
geezer 'You got to use flies — —' / The first guy makes his
move only the fly is too fast for him / I make the mistake of
snickering / He turns on me with a snarl / 'You interested in
our conversation?' The lady bartender comes hurrying over
/ 'You lookin' pretty good tonight, Erma' says the wino,
focussing on her jumbo breasts / 'Yeah, yeah,' she says 'I
always start lookin' good to you about this time' / 'I just don't
say nothin' earlier' he says / She laughs real loud / and
everybody up and down the bar he-haws / Even the huge
elk's head mounted on the wall seems to be snorting / The
barlady's breasts heave up and down in the heat / her gold
teeth shine and seem about to fall out on the counter as she

12

continues roaring / The jukebox suddenly adds its voice and it's Johnny Cash in his element two thousand miles from home / The barlady breathes in my ear hoarsely 'Have another beer deerie' / I do / The barlady throws her head back again / There is a far off roaring as of the sea. . . .

*Rogue River / NW of Grants Pass / Tuesday 9 Aug 77*

A fifteen year old boy drowned here yesterday / swept away by the undercurrent / his boots on / sucked into a deep hole / We found a striped T-shirt and a pair of canvas shoes upon a beach downriver / Looked more like girls' shoes but might have been boys' if he were slightly androgynous /
We turned them over to the county sheriff / who came zooming downriver / in a tin boat / with his emblem emblazoned on the bow / We didn't mention androgyny.

*10 August '77*

Raft trip today / Up early to ride in a truck upriver to the starting point / The drought has reduced the size of the river by half / but still plenty of water / with rapids and deep pools full of sharp boulders and whirling funnels of white water / Too much sun, more than 100F out on the river / We shoot the first rapids in the rubber raft, get hung up between boulders in the middle of a riffle, lose an oar, get loose and recover it, go on to Galice / And on down, as on a rollercoaster, laughing & shouting, some hilarious god in charge of us. . . .

*11 August 77*

We are lost by the river / in stone solitude / only the sound of the river / to save us / from total stillness / from the total void / even the water only earth's breath / Nothing happening / nothing stirring / as if life itself had yet to begin / or were all over forever / Nirvana — or Samsara — or only the total boredom of the boondocks / We are saved / by a big recreational vehicle camper / that backs down the beach road / and parks almost on top of us / ladies in plastic haircurlers and little fuckers bearing plastic pails / bursting from it / screeching to the beach.

# BEFORE DAWN

The enormous egrets before dawn
                              fishing the river
            sailing along so elegantly
                        like great gliders
                              sleek airliners
                                 noiseless
            long necks extended
                  long legs retracted
                        straight back

gliding straight above the waters — —
                        white water caps
                              they look into
                  for whatever survivors
                        of the great drought
            Water too warm
                        Fish gone
                              dead & washed away
                  to sea sixty miles away

A big hawk swoops down
                        like a dive bomber stalled
            The egret
                  as suddenly pulls up
                              in a steep climb

and in an instant so gracefully
                    folds itself & lands
          on a high peak of rock
                    beak bared to the hawk
The sun
      still does not
                dare to come up
        The black hawk
                like a shadow of himself
                              sinks away

# SPIDER DAWN

The sun is coming at last
  A spider draws the light
                          with his web
        through dawn's windows

He can drop on you like a parachutist
  like a highwire artist
    zooming down a line

Black and poisonous the Black Widows
                  can kill you in an hour
You'd lie there writhing and puking
    No use to get up
             they've got you
 like we got them so often
              Just lie there & writhe
                and double up finally
                   rigor mortis
     like a crumpled bug
          croaking on DDT
   or a crooked-up snake
              stung by a scorpion

Just lie there in total agony!

The sun is coming through
                    the windows of dawn
The spider will draw you up
                    into his web
          before the sun
                    can carry you Away

# READING APOLLINAIRE
# BY THE ROGUE RIVER

Reading Apollinaire here
sitting crosslegged
on sleepingbag & poncho
in the shadow of a huge hill
before the sun clears it
Woke up early on the shore
and heard the river shushing
(like the sound a snake might make
sliding over riprap
if you magnified the sound)
My head still down upon the ground
one eye without perspective
sees the stream sliding by
through the sand
as in a desert landscape
Like a huge green watersnake
with white water markings
the river slithers by
and where the canyon turns
and the river drops from sight
seems like a snake about to disappear
down a deep hole
Indians made their myths
of this great watersnake

slid down from mountains far away
And I see the Rogue for real
as the Indians saw him
the Rogue all wild white water
a cold-blooded creature
drowning and dousing
the Rogue ruler of the land
transforming it at will
with a will of its own
a creature to be feared and respected
pillaging its way to the sea
with great gravity
still ruled by that gravity
which still rules all
so that we might almost say
Gravity is God
manifesting Himself
as Great God Sun
who will one day make Himself
into a black hole in space
who will one day implode Himself
into Nothing
All of which the slithering Rogue
knows nothing of
in its headlong
blind rush to the sea
And though its head
is already being eaten

by that most cruel and churning
monster Ocean
the tail of the snake
knows it not
and continues turning & turning
toward its final hole
and toward that final black hole
into which all some day
will be sucked burning

As I sit reading a French poet
    whose most famous poem is about
        the river that runs through the city
           taking time & life & lovers with it
          And none returning
                none returning

# THE FATE OF THE POET

Apollinaire looks up at me
        from the cover of his book
                lying on my sleepingbag

His derby says
                'Selected Writings'
                        on its crown

His neck is tight
                in a white
                        debonaire collar

His eyes are
        black bees

His scraggly black moustache
                covers the crack of his mouth
    like a nest of black ants
        in the white sand of his face

He
    will never
                speak again

# HORSES AT DAWN

The horses the horses the wild horses at dawn
as in a watercolor by Ben Shahn
they are alive in the high meadow
in the high country on the far mesa
you can see them galloping
you can see them snorting
you can hear their thunder distantly
you can hear the small thunder
of their small hooves
insistently
like wood hammers thrumming
on a distant drum
The sun roars &
throws their shadows
out of the night

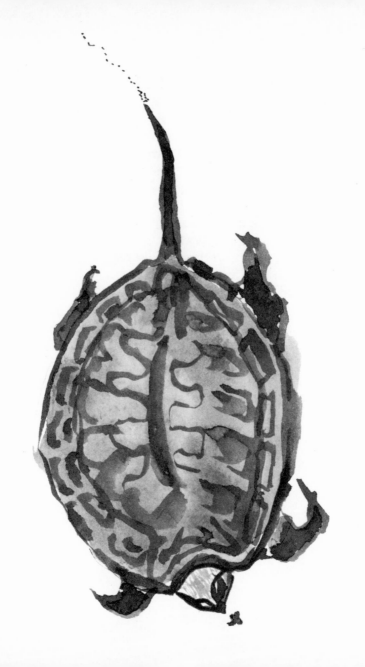

*13 August 77*
*Siskiyou National Forest*


I put on the diving mask and went down / A few feet below
the surface a few minnows circled me / A little further down a
few small trout no more than three inches/ I lie motionless
just below the surface and search the deepest part of the
pool / There at the very bottom between boulders / in the
very deepest hole / I suddenly spy him / a huge fat grey
speckled trout / perhaps eight pounds / perfectly still against
the grey rocks / He would have been invisible from the surface / and invisible without the mask / Then suddenly I saw
another fat speckled trout / not quite as big / quite close to
the first / almost like his shadow / or her shadow / this one
too perfectly motionless / as if not even breathing / though
the swift stream poured by above it / Summer of the great
drought / and this the only deep pool left / in this part of
what had been a small river / now most of the streambed
exposed / fifty feet of boulders and small rocks and gravel /
the stream itself shrunk to a width of twenty feet / The pool
isolated by rapids at each end / no more than two inches of
water going over at any one spot / Last season the two fish
must have made it up this far / then the stream shrunk still
more / and here they were caught / in the shrinking hole /
now no more than eight feet deep / where they lay motionless / waiting / trapped / their world shrinking and shrinking /

Still they lie at the bottom / very still / conserving what they've got / They are fat from feeding on all the other dammed-up stream life around them / periwinkles / tiny minnows / crawdads and bugs / skeeters and tiny transparent wigglers that look like floating questionmarks / They are full and don't bite at anything / don't go for lures worms salmoneggs or bread / Fishermen don't have divingmasks and never see them down there and pass on quickly / as we dive down again & again / and see the fish in their steady-state of meditation / a final yoga discipline / which could go on until there is no water at all left in the stream / Then we might find them / still in swimming position / fins extended / mouth slightly open / eyes half closed / Or still later we might find their skeletons intact / in the same positions / baked in the firey sun / like Buddhist monks burned alive in lotus positions / Or still much later another age might discover / two fossil skeletons / imprinted on the boulders / at the very bottom of the crypt / as evidence of some former strange form / of a thing called Life / And if we stayed on here with them / waiting & waiting / that later age / might also not be able to imagine one boy and his father fishing / by this stream / though our two round skulls be found / with the fishes / Yet seeing now the beauty of those fish / down there below the surface / so still and lovely / in their deep dream / dappled in their last deep pool / We fish no longer / turn / and go on / into the deeper pools / of our own lives.

# AT THE PUBLIC MARKET

At the Public Market
Seattle wintertime
A big shaggy bearded man
like Walt Whitman
standing still in the cold rain
with his shivering dog
a cardboard sign on him:

I AM OVER 70
MY DOG HAS THREE LEGS
NOBODY
WANTS US

The hard rain pours down
There is no tin cup

*12/12/77*

# CLAMSHELL ALLIANCE

Here by the sea
    Vashon Island Puget Sound
 at the Portage
     lie in bed
       thinking what to do
'The sea
  is calm tonight'
Beneath it
  all not so calm
Nor inside us
    here at this isthmus
 this portage
    between two lives
 this isthmus
    built on Indian arrowheads
 all not so calm
We are all
   submerged in our lives
     in the 'bath of creation'
Yet the tide is full
The small clams and Quilcene oysters
    are their own alliance
     against the world's death
They are in league
   with the seas and the whales

They are in league
            with Moby Dick
                against the Ahabs of earth
The clams
            live and breathe closed up
We too
        close up tight on shore
                        clam up
                    hidden from ourselves
Yet here by the sea
                on Vashon
                        may open out
    in this summerhouse
                        as in a small Maine seaport
        or wherever — —
                    Vashon or Mannahatta — —
    the same salt tongue
                    licks us all
The stinging salt
        if we should open up
                        pours in
    but also the light
                    the lapped light of love. . .
        An illusion by the sea?
                        a romantic agony?
            a faint flickering
                        in the gloaming?

At the Coast Guard station
                    the great white lighthouse
                              still flashes all ways

## WRITTEN IN THE GREENPEACE 'DREAMBOOK'
(Aboard *Greenpeace VII* / Seattle-Vancouver Oct. 77)


Dreamt of
    Moby Dick the Great White Whale
        cruising about
           with a flag flying
               with an inscription on it
           "I Am what is left of Wild Nature"
    And Ahab pursuing in a jet boat with a ray gun
      and jet harpoons and super depth charges
      and napalm flamethrowers and electric
     underwater vibrators and the whole gory
       glorious efficient military-political-
           industrial-scientific tech-
          nology of the great-
         est civilisation the
        earth has ever
        known
       devoted to
     the absolute extinction and
   death of the natural world as we know it
And Captain Ahab   Captain Death   Captain Anti-Poetry
   Captain Dingbat No Face Captain Apocalypse
        at the helm
      of the killer ship of Death

And the blue-eyed whales

                            exhausted and running

    but still

             singing to each other. . .

# ROUGH NOTES FOR A ROUGH SONG OF ANIMALS DYING

In a dream within a dream I dreamt a dream
of reality
inside the ultimate computer
which is the universe
in which the Arrow of Time
flies both ways
through bent space
In a dream within a dream I dreamt
of all the animals dying
all animals everywhere
dying & dying
the wild animals the longhaired animals
winged animals feathered animals
clawed & scaled & furry animals
rutting & dying & dying
In a dream within a dream I dreamt
of creatures everywhere dying out
in shrinking rainforests
in piney woods & high sierras
on shrinking prairies & tumbleweed mesas
captured beaten trapped starved & stunned
cornered & traded
species not meant to be nomadic
wandering rootless as man

In a dream within a dream I dreamt
of all the animals crying out
in their hidden places
in the still silent places left to them
slinking away & crawling about
through the last wild places
through the dense underbrush
the last Great Thickets
beyond the mountains
crisscrossed with switchbacks
beyond the marshes
beyond the plains & fences
(the West won with barbed-wire machines)
in the high country
in the low country
crisscrossed with highways
In a dream within a dream I dreamt
of how they feed & rut & run & hide
In a dream within a dream I saw
how the seals are beaten on the ice-fields
the  soft white furry seals with eggshell skulls
the Great Green turtles beaten & eaten
exotic birds netted & caged & tethered
rare wild beasts & strange reptiles & weird woozoos
hunted down for zoos
by bearded blackmarketeers
who afterwards ride around Singapore
in German limousines with French whores

In a dream within a dream I dreamt
of the earth heating up & drying out
in the famous Greenhouse Effect
under its canopy of carbon dioxide
breathed out by a billion
infernal combustion engines
mixed with the sweet smell of burning flesh
In a dream within a dream I dreamt
of animals calling to each other
in codes we never understand
The seal and steer cry out
in the same voice
as they are clubbed
in Chicago stockyards & Newfoundland snowfields
It is the same cry
The wounds never heal
in the commonweal of animals
We steal their lives
to feed our own
and with their lives
our dreams are sown
In a dream within a dream I dreamt a dream
of the daily scrimmage for existence
in the wind-up model of the universe
the spinning meat-wheel world
in which I was a fish who eats his tail
in which I was a claw upon a beach

in which I was a snake upon a tree
in which I was a serpent's egg
a yin-yang yolk of good and evil
about to consume itself


*3/78*

# SUICIDE HAIKU

MAN FISHING
in shrinking gene pool
hooks last gene—
Jumps in

# CITY LIGHTS PUBLICATIONS

Artaud, Antonin. ANTHOLOGY.    $4.00

Beck, Julian. THE LIFE OF THE THEATRE.    $4.00

Bowen, Michael. JOURNEY TO NEPAL.    $2.50

Bowles, Paul. A HUNDRED CAMELS IN THE COURT-
YARD.    $1.50

Broughton, James. SEEING THE LIGHT.    $2.50

Brown, Governor Jerry, THOUGHTS.    $2.00

Bukowski, Charles. ERECTIONS, EJACULATIONS, EX-
HIBITIONS AND GENERAL TALES OF ORDINARY
MADNESS.    $5.95

Bukowski, Charles. NOTES OF A DIRTY OLD MAN.    $3.00

Burroughs, William. YAGE LETTERS.    $2.00

Cassady, Neal. THE FIRST THIRD.    $3.00

City Lights Journal No. 3.    $2.50

City Lights Journal No. 4.    $3.00

Corso, Gregory. GASOLINE and THE VESTAL
LADY.    $2.00

Cossery, Albert. MEN GOD FORGOT.    $1.50

David-Neel, Alexandra. SECRET ORAL TEACHINGS IN
TIBETAN BUDDHIST SECTS.    $2.50

diPrima, Diane. REVOLUTIONARY LETTERS.    $2.50

Dowden, George. BIBLIOGRAPHY OF ALLEN
GINSBERG. $17.50 (cloth)

Eberhardt, Isabelle. THE OBLIVION SEEKERS. $2.00

Fenollosa, Ernest. THE CHINESE WRITTEN CHARACTER
AS A MEDIUM FOR POETRY.    $2.50

Ferlinghetti. ed. CITY LIGHTS ANTHOLOGY.    $5.95

Ferlinghetti. PICTURES OF THE GONE WORLD.    $1.50

Genet, Jean. MAY DAY SPEECH.    $1.00

Ginsberg, Allen. CHICAGO TRIAL TESTIMONY.    $2.00

Ginsberg, Allen. THE FALL OF AMERICA.    $3.00

Ginsberg, Allen. HOWL AND OTHER POEMS.    $1.50

Ginsberg, Allen. INDIAN JOURNALS.    $3.00 / $6.50 (cloth)

Ginsberg, Allen. IRON HORSE.    $3.00

Ginsberg, Allen. KADDISH AND OTHER POEMS.   $2.50
Ginsberg, Allen. MIND BREATHS. $3.00 / $7.50 (cloth)
Ginsberg, Allen. PLANET NEWS. $2.50
Ginsberg, Allen. REALITY SANDWICHES.   $1.50
Hemingway, Ernest. COLLECTED POEMS. 50¢
Hirschman, Jack. LYRIPOL.   $2.50
Joyce, James. POMES PENYEACH.   $1.00
Kaufman, Bob. GOLDEN SARDINE.   $2.00
Kerouac, Jack. BOOK OF DREAMS.   $3.00
Kerouac, Jack. SCATTERED POEMS. $2.00
Lamantia, Philip. SELECTED POEMS.   $1.50
Lowry, Malcolm. SELECTED POEMS.   $1.50
Mailer, Norman. WHITE NEGRO.   $1.00
McClure, Michael. MEAT SCIENCE ESSAYS.   $1.95
Marx, Karl. LOVE POEMS.   $2.00
Michaux, Henri. MISERABLE MIRACLE.   $1.95
Moore, Daniel. BURNT HEART.   $2.50
Mrabet, Mohammed. M'HASHISH.   $1.50
Newton, Huey and Ericka Huggins. INSIGHTS &
      POEMS.   $2.00
Norse, Harold. HOTEL NIRVANA.   $2.00
O'Hara, Frank. LUNCH POEMS.   $2.00
Olson, Charles. CALL ME ISHMAEL.   $2.00
Parkinson, Tom. PROTECT THE EARTH.   $1.50
Patchen, Kenneth. LOVE POEMS.   $1.00
Patchen, Kenneth. POEMS OF HUMOR &
      PROTEST.   $1.50
Picasso, Pablo. HUNK OF SKIN.   $1.00
Pickard, Tom. GUTTERSNIPE.   $2.50
Plymell, Charles. LAST OF THE MOCCASINS.   $3.00
Pommy-Vega, Janine. POEMS TO FERNANDO.   $1.25
Prevert, Jacques. Paroles.   $1.50
Reed, John. ADVENTURES OF A YOUNG MAN.   $3.00
Rexroth, Kenneth. 30 SPANISH POEMS OF LOVE &
      EXILE.   $1.00
Richards, Charles & Janet. CHINESE COOKING.   $1.50
Sanders, Ed. INVESTIGATIVE POETRY.   $2.00

Smith, Paul Jordan. KEY TO THE ULYSSES OF JAMES
    JOYCE.   $1.50
Snyder, Gary. THE OLD WAYS.   $2.50
Solomon, Carl. MISHAPS PERHAPS. $1.50
Solomon, Carl. MORE MISHAPS. $1.50
Svevo, Italo. JAMES JOYCE. $1.25
Topor, Roland. PANIC.   $1.00
Upton, Charles. PANIC GRASS.   $1.00
Voznesensky, Andre. DOGALYPSE. $1.50
Waldman, Anne. FAST SPEAKING WOMAN.   $2.00
Waley, Arthur. THE NINE SONGS.   $2.50
Watts, Alan W. BEAT ZEN, SQUARE ZEN & ZEN.   $1.00
Whitman, Walt. AN AMERICAN PRIMER.   $1.50
Williams, William Carlos. KORA IN HELL:
    IMPROVISATIONS.   $2.00
Wilson, Colin. POETRY & MYSTICISM.   $2.00
Winslow, Pete. A DAISY IN THE MEMORY OF
    A SHARK.   $2.00
Yevtushenko, et al. RED CATS.   $1.00

## Also by Lawrence Ferlinghetti

## POETRY

*Pictures of the Gone World.* City Lights
*A Coney Island of the Mind.* New Directions
*Starting from San Francisco.* New Directions
*The Secret Meaning of Things.* New Directions
*Back Roads to Far Places.* New Directions
*Open Eye, Open Heart.* New Directions
*Who Are We Now?* New Directions

## PROSE

*Her.* New Directions
*The Mexican Night.* New Directions

## PLAYS

*Routines.* New Directions

## TRANSLATIONS

*Selections from Paroles*, Jacques Prévert. City Lights
*Dogalypse*, Andrei Voznesensky. City Lights